Grief

Discovery House Publishers

Books, music, and videos that feed the soul with the Word of God

Box 3566 Grand Rapids, MI 49501

Grief

*Comfort
for
Those
Who
Grieve
and
Those
Who
Want
to
Help*

Haddon W. Robinson
Illustrated by Nancy Munger

Grief

Copyright © 1996 by Haddon W. Robinson

Discovery House Publishers is affiliated with RBC Ministries, Grand Rapids, Michigan 49512.

Discovery House books are distributed to the trade by Thomas Nelson Publishers, Nashville, Tennessee 37214.

Unless otherwise indicated, Scripture is taken from the HOLY BIBLE: NEW INTERNATIONAL VERSION. Copyright © 1973, 1978, 1984 by the International Bible Society. Used by permission of Zondervan Bible Publishers.

Library of Congress Cataloging-in-Publication Data

Robinson, Haddon W.
    Grief : comfort for those who grieve and those who want to help / by Haddon W. Robinson.
        p.   cm.
    Originally published: Grand Rapids : Zondervan, 1974.
    ISBN 1-57293-010-1
    1. Grief—Religious aspects—Christianity. 2. Consolation. 3. Bereavement—Religious aspects—Christianity. I. Title.
BV4509.2.R62 1996
248.8'6—dc20   95-50812
                                                      CIP

Printed in the United States of America

96 97 98 99 00 01 / CHG / 10 9 8 7 6 5 4 3 2 1

Contents

Beggars in Search of Comfort

"Have you ever grieved?"

The question caught me by surprise. It was asked by a gentleman in his eighties who had just lost his wife of sixty-three years.

It was hard to answer. Grief is painful. Thinking about it reminds us that we don't control what happens to us. It reminds us, as well, of many things we have tried to forget. Grief hurts too much to keep it on the front burners of our minds.

Of course I have grieved. My mother died when I was eleven. She had been in the hospital for two years before her death. I had learned to live apart from her, but when she died I had to live without her. I still remember her funeral, the smell of the flowers in the mortuary, and even a fragment of what the preacher talked about that afternoon. I remember my father sobbing. I had never seen him cry before. While I can't bring to mind much that happened after my mother's death, I had to cope. For a year or more, especially in the evenings, I felt a lonesome pain that wouldn't go away. For months my grades took a beating in school.

Years later I grieved when my father passed way. He was eighty-eight; it was time for him to go. When we buried him in Texas, he was far from the few friends he had left in New York City where he had spent his adult life. As I stood by his grave I wanted to shout at the cars rushing past on the highway beyond the iron fence, "Stop! Stop! A good man has died and no one seems to care. Stop and notice!" But the traffic kept whizzing by. For several days after his death, when I was alone in my office or driving in my car, I broke down in sobs to my surprise.

I grieved with a couple whose five-year-old son, Matt, was killed in a freak hunting accident. His father's rifle discharged as he was maneuvering through a wire fence. The bullet hit the boy, and the lad crumpled to the ground and died in an instant. I served as their pastor. I spent hours with that couple. I conducted Matt's funeral and stood with the parents at the graveside. It was a bleak winter day, yet I don't suppose a bright spring day would have made much difference. For weeks I felt the pain, and I could not shake it.

"Have you ever grieved?" Of course I have. So have you.

Everyone experiences grief. "The statistics on death are quite impressive," George Bernard Shaw observed, "One out of one people die." Since death is a part of life, and grief follows death, then grief is universal. No one escapes it.

Grief isn't limited to death. We experience this emotion, or a complex of emotions, whenever we lose anyone or anything we care about deeply. An amputee after losing an arm or leg goes through grief. When you load all your belongings into a U-Haul van and kiss your family good-bye, grief sometimes makes the trip with you. A young woman grieves when she breaks up with her boyfriend; and in later years, a wife grieves when she divorces her husband. A worker may leave a long-held job with a pink slip or a gold watch, but in either case that employee feels a deep sense of grief. Parents often experience grief when their daughter goes off to college or a son leaves to join the Navy. Whenever we lose any person or possession that has given us emotional security or satisfaction, we will grieve.

All of us, therefore, will go through grief. Perhaps you are grieving now.

An old nursery rhyme reminds us that we live in the company of beggars:

Hark! Hark! The dogs do bark,
The beggars are coming to town;
Some in rags, some in tags,
And some in velvet gowns.

All around us there are men and women, old and young, who are suffering grief. Sometimes their grief is as obvious as a tear. At other times they disguise their grief with activity, or smiles, or beautiful make-up jobs. They are beggars in need of comfort. And at some time, as sure as loss and death, you and I will be beggars ourselves.

How, then, can we cope when grief descends upon us? How can we comfort others who mourn? Not all grief is the same. There is "good grief" and there is "bad grief," constructive or destructive ways of handling our pain.

Strangely enough, although grief lays its hand on all of us, we know relatively little about how people experience it. All grief is intensely personal. No one has walked your exact path before. Many writers have opened up their lives to give us a glimpse of their pain when they have lost someone dear to them. Those books tell us a great deal, but they are always someone else's journey.

Grief is difficult to study. Sociologists and psychiatrists have been understandably reluctant to break in on mourners to ask questions or make films of how grief works. Grief is a companion of death, and in our culture death has few students. Since social scientists are not immune from the uneasiness of their culture, to some extent, death and therefore grief is for them a forbidden topic.

Although death is a "taboo" subject, some have ventured to study it. One of these attempts took place in the 1940s. Dr. Erich Lindeman, a professor of psychiatry at Harvard University, worked with relatives and close friends of those killed in Boston's Coconut Grove nightclub fire. From his observations Lindeman concluded that grief suffering cannot be avoided, and the bereaved must enter into it and work through it in order to experience "good grief." He called this process "grief work." Through grief work the sufferers must be set free from "bondage" to all they have lost so that they can live with the memories, the hurts, the joys, and sorrows that remain a part of their lives. Lindeman maintained that mourners never escape the process nor can they break free until they have worked through their grief. While they may never get over the loss, by doing grief work they can get through it.

Jesus in His introduction to the Sermon on the Mount declared, "Blessed are those who mourn, for they shall be comforted." To be comforted in the face of grief, we must mourn. If we refuse to deal with our grief, then "good grief" turns into "bad grief."

How "Good Grief" Becomes "Bad Grief." One common way people have dealt with grief is to avoid it. This response is as old as history. Centuries ago the Stoics taught their disciples not to mourn. The best way to respond to grief, they said, was to deny it. Many sincere men and women carry on that stoic tradition.

From their earliest years young men are told, "Big boys don't cry." A youngster may first be taught that lesson when he falls from a swing, and in fright and pain begins to cry. When his mother consoles him, she may whisper, "There, there, everything's all right. Don't cry. Big boys don't cry." By the time the boy is ten he is convinced that tears and manliness don't mix. By the time he reaches eighteen, he wouldn't think of weeping, even though he has been jilted by his girlfriend. At fifty, he may not know how to cry at all.

Women, too, may be taught that weeping is weakness. During their growing-up years and afterward, they may have been put down when they burst into tears. As a result, they are conditioned to feel embarrassed when they weep. To be strong is to be a stoic. After a funeral, friends may remark about a widow whose world has been shattered and whose heart is breaking, "Look at how brave she is—she didn't shed a tear!" But courage and tears are not opposites. Weeping is a language of the soul.

Doesn't Faith Dry All Tears? Religious people sometimes mishandle their own grief and the grief of others by thinking that faith and tears don't mix. A sturdy faith in God and a firm belief in the promise of life eternal, they reason, should keep us from weeping or giving way to grief. But grief is not a denial of faith. The shortest verse in the Bible is found in John 11:35. It states simply: "Jesus wept."

Those two words speak volumes about Jesus' inner feelings and His willingness to express His grief.

Those two words describe what happened after the funeral of Lazarus, a beloved friend of Jesus.

Mary, Lazarus' sister, fell at Jesus' feet and out of a broken heart said, "Lord, if you had been here, my brother would not have died." Jesus, deeply moved asked, "Where have you laid him?"

Then Mary and her sister, Martha, and the people in the village made their way to the town cemetery. Jesus stood in front of the tomb of Lazarus, and the biblical writer states simply, "Jesus wept." Seeing the tears trickling down his cheeks, friends of the family remarked, "See how he loved him!"

He who remains history's greatest and most complete person stood by the graveside of a good friend and wept. In that incident Jesus with His tears destroyed the notion that "big boys don't cry."

Christians who believe that tears are incompatible with faith may also have misunderstood a sentence Paul wrote to his friends in the city of Thessalonica. To those who had lost their loved ones, he explained, "Brothers, we do not want you to be ignorant about those who fall asleep, or to grieve like the rest of men, who have no hope" (1 Thessalonians 4:13).

Unfortunately, some reading those words have struggled under "bad grief" because they have left off the last phrase of Paul's sentence. The apostle wasn't telling his readers not to grieve. Grief is as common as being human. After all, grief is an emotion like love, fear, guilt, or anger and is probably a mixture of all of these. Our Christian faith does not provide immunity from emotions, and it is as futile to deny grief as it would be to deny laughter. But rather Paul was telling his Christian friends not to grieve as unbelievers do who possess no hope. Our faith can keep grief from overwhelming us, but God rewards no crowns because we refuse to weep.

Strange and unpredictable things happen to those who do not face their losses and work through their grief. A fourteen-year-old boy has struggled with depression since he was seven. He is the victim of a divorce and feels like a pawn in his parents' chess game. He has been shuttled between father and mother, both of whom he loves, but he has never felt fully at home in either of their houses. Neither he nor his parents can make sense out of his sudden outbursts of anger, his truancy, and shoplifting. The young man has not dealt with his grief.

A paraplegic talks about riding his motorcycle again. His young wife who has married him "for better or for worse" wants to love him and help him. She doesn't understand the fury he spews out at her. He simply will not accept the reality of his loss. She is frightened that she has lost him. Both husband and wife struggle with their grief.

It is only as we work through our own grief and help others to do so that grief can become "good grief." Grief is a part of life, and God has given us tear ducts to allow us to express our sorrow.

We need to know how to turn bad grief into good grief for ourselves and for others.

The Stages of Grief

What do people suffering grief go through when they lose someone who has meant the world to them, someone, perhaps, who has been a pillar or a pillow in their lives? What can we do to help friends burdened down with grief? While grief is not limited to death, these questions may find their clearest answers if we consider how we experience grief when confronted with the death of someone we love.

There are at least three different stages people move through as they grieve. Not everyone experience each stage with the same intensity, and the time spent in each stage will vary with each person and the nature of the loss. For instance, the loss of a child will usually create a deeper and longer experience of grief than the loss of an aged parent.

As people navigate each stage of grief, the principle for a successful journey is the same: grief needs to be expressed. Grief resembles steam in an engine. Unless the steam can escape in a controlled manner, pressure builds up and the boiler explodes. Grief work, too, must be done. It will be done.

Sooner or later, correctly or incorrectly, completely or incompletely, in a positive or a distorted manner, the painful work will take place. Therefore, we should encourage hurting friends to express their grief, and when we go through that dark valley ourselves we must give expression to our feelings. Through emotional release grief sufferers actualize and accept their loss, and the intellectual awareness that they have lost someone precious to them, then becomes a knowing in their souls.

The Crisis Stage

The first stage of grief may be called the "crisis" stage. In the case of death this is the period immediately after receiving the news that someone dear has died. During this crisis stage a grieving person may go through a series of different emotions. The first is often shock and surprise. If death comes suddenly, it hits like a hammer blow. Even when the death has been expected, it has finally happened and those who are bereaved can be physically shaken when informed of the death. Instinctively, people may deny death. "Oh no!" they exclaim because they cannot take it in. At that point, numbness may come like an anesthesia to the mind. Usually, there is also an emotional release, and the bereaved breaks down and weeps. For some the crying is done within a circle of friends; for others it is better done alone. Tranquilizers and sleeping pills should be used sparingly during this stage of mourning because weeping is an effective medicine for the spirit.

The ministry of friends. What can friends do during the crisis stage to help grief sufferers accept and actualize their loss? Above all, friends should be there. People suffering grief need to know that they are not alone. As needs arise, friends can take care of them. Baby-sitting, phone calls, food, laundry, errands, transportation, and scores of the other details of living may be overlooked unless a friend steps in.

Friends also listen. While it is important to lend a hand, close friends also give an ear. A grieving person often wants to talk about death, but such talk may make others feel uncomfortable. Because of that, some people are tempted to change the subject to get the grief sufferer to "think about something else." But there is nothing else to talk about that matters. A good listener gives the grief sufferer permission to express thoughts and feelings by asking, "Tell me how things are." Or, "Would you like to talk about it?" Those who hurt often want to repeat what went on just before and after they heard the shocking news. That is healthy, for that is how people come to accept the reality of what has happened. Sometimes the details are related again and again, and it is a loving act to listen thoughtfully. Of course, a good friend also respects the need for silence and for privacy and will not force a conversation that is not wanted.

When we listen we ought not be surprised at what seem like "way out thoughts." Some grieving people escape into fantasy because reality crushes them. They may talk as though the death has not taken place or act as though they are in a trance. They may nurse a secret hope that they are having a bad dream and that their loved one will return. They may even start to prepare a meal for someone who will never sit at their table again. Although such fantasies should not surprise us, we should not support them. In a kind and gentle manner we need to encourage grief sufferers to face reality. It is both false and futile to deny that death has taken place.

Unfortunately, although listening is essential in the crisis stage, we are tempted to talk too much and listen too little. When we are uncomfortable with grief we feel that we have to say something. Religious people struggle to say something Christian. "She is at home with the Lord." "God must have loved him to take him so young." "Jim is better off in heaven." "He wouldn't want to come back." All of these platitudes may be true but they seldom provide much comfort. After all, people grieve not for the loved one who has died but for themselves and the loss they have sustained. A brief, honest expression of how we feel, free of pious phrases, can be offered if a grieving person opens up, but generally our presence speaks more than our words.

Joseph Bayly in his helpful book, *The Last Thing We Talk About: Help and Hope for Those Who Grieve,* shares an experience of comfort he received when one of his children died. "I was sitting," he remembered, "torn by grief. Someone came and talked to me of God's dealings, of why it happened, of hope beyond the grave. He talked constantly; he said things I knew were true."

"I was unmoved, except to wish he would go away. He finally did.

"Another came and sat beside me. He didn't talk. He didn't ask leading questions. He just sat beside me for an hour or more, listened when I said something, answered briefly, prayed simply, left.

"I was moved. I was comforted. I hated to see him go."

The Crucible Stage

The second stage of grief is the "crucible" stage. Often, this phase lasts three months or longer, and it is most intense during the first six weeks after the funeral. During this time the grief sufferer must weaken and break the emotional ties with the past, and with any plans for the future which are bound up with the person who has died. The process is painful, but it must be done. As in *Gulliver's Travels,* where Gulliver is pinned to the earth by the stakes and ropes of the Lilliputians, so a grief sufferer, too, is bound by a thousand emotional cords to the loved one who is gone.

During the crucible stage people experience a variety of emotions and reactions. It is not unusual for grief sufferers to be so completely smothered by depression that they worry about losing their sanity. They often feel isolated and cut off from others since family and friends who gave themselves so generously during the first stage of grief have gotten caught up again with the business of life. Sometimes weeks—even months—go by while a desperate loneliness or an unremitting emptiness overwhelms the mourner.

C. S. Lewis wrote after the death of his wife, "No one ever told me that grief felt so like fear. I am not afraid, but the sensation is like being afraid; the same fluttering in the stomach, the same restlessness, the yawning. I keep on swallowing."

Edna St. Vincent Millay in her poem, "Lament," expressed similar feelings.

> Life must go on,
> And the dead be forgotten.
> Life must go on,
> Though good men die.
>
> Anne, eat your breakfast;
> Dan, take your medicine;
> Life must go on,
> I forget just why.

Guilt and grief are often companions. Sometimes grief and guilt go hand-in-hand because of what the grief sufferer did or did not do during the final illness. At other times it is guilt over all the "shoulds" of a lifetime. In life there is always another day, but with death comes finality. Others grieve that they have not been perfect, and they focus on unkind words or inconsiderate acts they wish they could take back.

It is not unusual for grief-bearers to wrestle with unfounded sensations of guilt. They have given their grief a wrong label. When we go through any painful situation over which we have no control, we may blame ourselves. Parents feel guilty if their child dies of cancer; survivors of plane wrecks feel guilty that they were spared and others killed. Somehow assuming blame gives us the impression that we do have a handle on life. We would rather feel guilty than helpless. False guilt is a deception of the mind that we must unmask and recognize for what it is.

Some guilt, however, is real. For guilt that has stained our souls, it is helpful to remember that because Jesus suffered hell for us, there is forgiveness with God—complete forgiveness—for all our sins. Real guilt requires real repentance, and while it may be difficult to do, we must accept God's forgiveness. It has been provided for us at an enormous price. Because of His forgiveness we can forgive ourselves.

Hostility often rises to the surface. During the crucible stage of grief people become angry—angry at life, death, God, and even at the deceased. A young wife burst out in anger after her husband had been killed in an automobile accident. "Why did he do this to me?" Because such anger makes no sense, mourners often look for a scapegoat. They may lash out at the attending physician who didn't do enough, or at the pastor who didn't visit enough, or at friends who didn't care enough.

If such anger is directed at us, we ought to absorb it. Arguing or defending ourselves can increase the sufferer's sense of guilt and make the emotions more difficult to express. When the hostility is expressed at others, we can respond with a simple statement of fact. "From what I observed, the pastor did all he could." Perhaps at some later time when life has become more stable, it might be helpful to discuss the matter in a more probing way.

How friends can help. What specific things can we do during this crucible stage to help grief sufferers actualize their loss? Once again, we can be there. Immediately after the death, people's

sympathy and help flow like a river. But a month, two months, sometimes six months later loneliness and loss often make their strongest impact. During those months, when others have forgotten what the grief sufferer can never forget, friends are needed more than ever.

Late afternoons and evenings are particularly difficult. Dinner hours, which may have been occasions for conversation, can be especially lonely. Thoughtful friends understand that. They will extend dinner invitations and make them specific to show that the invitation is genuine. "We'd love to have you join us for dinner on Friday evening. We'll set a place for you. You can stay or go as you please."

Providing a ride to church or to a shopping center shows concern. Taking a child who has lost a parent to a circus or a ball game demonstrates love; likewise cutting the lawn or shoveling snow for a widow can ease her burden. Including a widow on the guest list for dinner parties is an important act of grace. Many women who are widows feel that they have lost not only their husbands but also their circle of old friends.

During those days we can also listen. The person in grief often wants and needs to talk about memories or to simply sit with a good friend. A little girl lost a playmate in death, and one day reported to her family that she had gone to comfort the sorrowing mother. "What did you say?" the father asked. "Nothing," the child replied, "I just climbed up on her lap and cried with her."

When visiting those working through grief, we may be reluctant to mention the person who has died, thinking that our comments will only open wounds. Seldom is that true. Reflecting on a conversation or a happy incident from the past can show that we, too, have loved and miss the person who has died.

Thus, we should allow and encourage grief sufferers to express their feelings and their memories if they want to do so. Some feel comfortable talking and sharing their thoughts and recollections. Others may resort to writing. C. S. Lewis wrestled with his grief by putting his reflections into a series of journals, which were later published as *A Grief Observed.* One minister asks people to write down all the ways in which their everyday life has been changed because of their loss. Although it is painful, the exercise forces the grief sufferer to think and feel each loss. The pain is part of the healing.

Others find help in reading. We find courage and hope in discovering that others have traveled a similar path and have found a clearing. Catherine Marshall wrote about her grief in *To Live Again*; Joseph Bayly, who lost three children to death provides perspective in *The Last Thing We Talk About: Help and Hope for Those Who Grieve*; and Bea Decker helps with the special problems of widowhood in *After the Flowers Have Gone.* Nicholas Wolterstorff offers a deeply sensitive account of a parent's heartbreak and healing in *Lament for a Son.* Lloyd and Gwendolyn Carr in their *Fierce Goodbye* write about finding hope in spite of their despair over a daughter's suicide. Harold Dosterveen in *Too Early Frost* reflects on the agony his family experienced in losing a child to cancer. Meg Woodson, who suffered multiple losses, describes how she learned to live through the holidays and special days of the year in *The Toughest Days of Grief.* Bob Deitz in *Life After*

Loss supplies an extended discussion about going on when everything within you is calling it quits.

While brief drop-in visits can help people in this crucible phase of grief, pastors or close friends should also consider scheduling formal times for check-up visits. For example, schedule an appointment once each week for the first month; every other week for the next three months; and then once a month for the rest of the year. Whatever schedule is arranged is better than the broad invitation, "Call me if you need help." Those offers, while well intentioned, are too vague to be accepted.

The Construction Stage

The third stage of grief is the "construction" stage in which the grief sufferer recreates new patterns for living that are not emotionally tied to the past. Mourners need encouragement to move out into life again as soon as they have the emotional and spiritual energy to do so. Activities should not become distractions to keep the bereaved from working through grief; instead they should be the natural result of having faced it. C. S. Lewis talked about "the laziness of grief," and it may be necessary to gently press friends to move out into a more active life while not insisting they do so. Through such encouragement we may help them live again.

Some people begin to put their lives together by finding a job. Many people have to return to work, and others have to enter the marketplace for the first time. Some men and women who have no financial concerns invest themselves in others by volunteering to work at their church or in their community. Many have enrolled in a college or a seminary or a business school to learn new things or to establish fresh, creative patterns for living again.

Guarding the Center of Life

"Watch for falling rocks." Signs with those words admonish drivers on mountain roads in the Pacific Northwest. These signs seem like an exercise in futility. Should heavy burdens tumble down the mountainside, drivers, no matter how aware, could not escape them. Precautions against falling rocks must be taken before they fall.

Be Aware of the Way Grief Works

Therefore, what can we do to guard against the impact of grief before it smashes in on top of us? First, we can become aware of how grief works. Understanding what happens during the stages of grief, why people feel and act as they do, may make us less vulnerable to the ravages of grief. We are less likely to be shocked, or terrified, or rendered helpless by the crush of unexpected emotions. Grief always brings pain which cannot be avoided; but the hurt may be lessened if we comprehend what is taking place.

Guard Today's Relationships with Care

In addition, we can protect our relationships with those we love. Regret is the stepchild of grief. Looking back through tears people often feel remorse for harsh words spoken, for kindnesses left undone, for opportunities to express love not taken, or for conversations stifled by life's busy-ness. Samuel Rogers spoke of the anguish of regret in his *Reflections*:

> For who, alas! has lived.
> Nor in the watches of the night recalled
> Word, he has wished unsaid and deeds
>   undone.

To live in love today can help you live without regret in some dark tomorrow.

Find a Firm Center for Life

Guard the center of life. Undoubtedly, the harshest grief comes when the core of life has been shattered. Our lives resemble a wheel—what is put at the hub holds the spokes together. Some people live for possessions.

Wealth can so possess people that everything—family, church, occupation, recreation, friendships—is governed by that center. If a depression wipes out savings and investments, then life crumbles.

Power, the heady delight of controlling people and institutions, may form the hub of life. Everything is centered on gaining more power. Then an election is lost, or a promotion goes to someone else, or a position is phased out, and the resulting grief can overwhelm someone stripped of their reason for living.

People, too, can become a wobbly center for our lives. A family can become the major reason for living. Our existence may gain its color and its strength from our spouses or our children. Indeed, wives and husbands and children make good spokes but terrible hubs. When a partner dies or children are taken from us, we may be devastated because they alone were all that really mattered.

Jesus Christ—The Eternal Center

Grief is tempered if you have an eternal center for your life. The good news of the Bible is simply this: you may have a relationship with the eternal God by centering your life on Jesus Christ. Putting it another way, Jesus Himself can become the hub of your life.

"There is nothing in the Gospels more significant than the way in which Jesus deliberately places Himself at the center of His message," Dr. James Stewart, the noted Scottish theologian, observed about Christ. "He does not say with other teachers, 'the truth is everything, I am nothing.' He declares, 'I am the truth.'. . . He does not offer the guidance of a code or a philosophy to guide men through the uncertainties of an unknown future; He says, 'I am with you always, to the end of the age.' "

David, a powerful and well-loved king of Israel testified in Psalm 23, "Even though I walk through the valley of the shadow of death, I will

fear no evil, for you are with me." Like David, in that personal and intimate relationship with God, experienced by multitudes of men and women, you can find a hub for your life that nothing can destroy.

Paul, who throughout his life struggled through overwhelming hardship and loss, nevertheless affirmed:

> I have become absolutely convinced that neither death nor life, neither messenger of heaven nor monarch of earth, neither what happens today nor what may happen tomorrow, neither a power from on high nor a power from below, nor anything else in God's whole world has any power to separate us from the love of God in Christ Jesus our Lord! (Romans 8:38-39, PHILLIPS).

Christians with this unflinching faith in the sovereign God do not deny grief. But even in their darkest, most wrenching hours, they borrow God's strength. In their tears and pain they cling to God who will never let them go. What the Savior has done for others He will do for you. When you are shaken, and you know that life will never be the same again, you can trust and not be afraid. You can live in hope with the sturdy confidence that God will dry your tears and put you on your feet again.

Note to the Reader

The publisher invites you to share your response to
the message of this book by writing Discovery House
Publishers, Box 3566, Grand Rapids, MI 49501, USA. For
information about other Discovery House books, music,
or videos, contact us at the same address or call 1-800-
653-8333. Find us on the Internet at http://www.dhp.org/
or send e-mail to books@dhp.org.